# Who Was
# Annie Oakley?

By Stephanie Spinner
Illustrated by Larry Day

Grosset & Dunlap • New York

# Contents

# Who Was Annie Oakley?

*"Aim at a high mark, and you'll hit it."*

—Annie Oakley

Who was Annie Oakley?

Her real name was Phoebe Ann Moses, and she ignored rules all her life. In an age when ladies did not handle guns, she became a sharpshooting legend. While most women stayed at home with their children, she traveled the world performing for enormous crowds, living happily in a big canvas tent. She was quiet, even shy, yet a brilliant performer.

During her lifetime, 1860–1926, women were paid far less than men, but at her peak she earned as much as the President of the United States. She was one of the best-known women of her age, and the public loved her, yet she was never anything but modest and down-to-earth.

Her life story inspired books, movies, television shows, and Broadway musicals. Most important, it changed the image of American women forever.

# Chapter 1
# Darke County

Phoebe Ann Moses was born on August 13, 1860, in Darke County, Ohio. Her birthplace—a rough settler's cabin built by her father, Jacob—was near the tiny village of Woodland. It was also

close enough to the woods for good hunting. Even as a tiny girl, Annie loved to go hunting with her father.

Sadly, Jacob Moses died of pneumonia when Annie was five years old. He left her mother, Susan, with six young children to care for. Susan Moses was a hardworking country nurse. But her wages—$1.25 a week— were not nearly enough to feed and clothe the family. They were very poor.

Annie and her brother and sisters helped out as best they could. They cared for the animals, did the laundry, worked in the garden, baked and cooked and sewed, and looked after the babies. "Somehow we managed to struggle along," Annie said of those times.

Annie always liked roaming in the woods. They were alive with squirrels, rabbits, chipmunks, turkeys, and pheasants. She began making traps—cornstalks stacked up and tied with string—to catch wild birds. Her father had taught her how to make them, and she was good at it.

Her traps put food on the table every day. "We served them toasted with dressing, fried, broiled, fricasseed, and in potpies, and sometimes they made a nourishing broth," Annie wrote of the birds she caught.

As welcome as the food was, Susan Moses found Annie's hunting troubling. She wanted her daughter to be a lady, not

a hunter. Moreover, Susan was a Quaker. She
believed in living without harming others. She had

forbidden Annie to touch Jacob's rifle, which hung over the fireplace.

Annie had never shot a gun. But she had watched her father many times. One day when she was alone, she climbed on a chair and took down the rifle. She knew she was disobeying her mother. She also knew her brothers and sisters were nearly sick with hunger.

Somehow Annie managed to load and fire the big old rifle, and to hit a squirrel. When she brought it home, Susan Moses was pleased to have food for the family. But she was also disturbed by Annie's growing interest in guns. They might be necessary for survival, but they were dangerous. Susan Moses did not like them.

Annie felt differently. "I guess the love of the gun must have been born in me," she said. By the time she was ten, she was handling her father's rifle with ease.

# Chapter 2
# The Infirmary

In 1871, Annie was sent to work at the Darke County Infirmary. This was a poorhouse—a place for orphans and homeless poor people who couldn't take care of themselves.

Annie did housework in exchange for room and board. If she wanted to earn a little money, she could mend and sew.

Though she was not happy about living there,

Annie understood why her mother had sent her away. Susan Moses was haunted by the fear that she could not provide for her children. Sending children to other households was a common practice at the time, a way to ensure that they would be cared for. Annie's younger sister Hulda already was living with another family.

Things started off well enough at the infirmary. Annie learned to knit and embroider and use a sewing machine. Samuel and Nancy Edington, the couple in charge, liked the way Annie always pitched in and did her best. They praised her for it.

Unfortunately, their praise reached the wrong ears. One day a man came to the infirmary looking for household help. He heard the Edingtons speak highly of Annie. So he offered her fifty cents a week, plus time off for school and hunting. His wife, he said, needed a baby-sitter for their newborn child.

Nancy Edington wrote to Susan Moses for permission to send Annie to this couple. Susan said yes, and Annie took the job.

For the next two years, Annie's life was miserable. The couple treated her so badly that she didn't even call them by name. To her they were "the wolves."

They worked her from early morning to late at night. They beat her. They refused to send her to school. They stole

Annie's letters from her mother. Not only that, they wrote to Susan Moses, saying that Annie was fine. Her mother never knew of Annie's ordeal.

One spring day when she was alone in the house, Annie realized she could run away. She gathered up her few belongings, hurried to the railroad station, and got on a train. She had forty-eight cents in her pocket—not nearly enough for her ticket. But a kindhearted passenger paid her fare, and soon she was home again.

# Chapter 3
# 25 Out of 25 Wins

Susan Moses had remarried before Annie went to the Darke County Infirmary. But her second husband fell ill and died. Once again the family had very little money. Annie decided to go back to the infirmary. It was not an easy decision for her, but she was determined to help out.

This time, encouraged by Nancy Edington, Annie practiced her reading and writing until she could do both without a struggle. The Edingtons put her in charge of the dairy. Its twelve cows supplied milk for the infirmary. Annie managed it so well that she got a raise.

"I saw to it that each tot had a glass of milk a day," Annie wrote with satisfaction.

Three years later, she returned home in time for her sister Lydia's wedding. It was a happy reunion. The wages Annie had sent to her mother—who now was married for the third time—had been a great help. Susan Moses was grateful to her daughter. Her criticism of Annie's shooting stopped. If her teenaged daughter was more interested in hunting than in marriage, so be it.

Soon Annie had won so many local turkey shoots—shooting contests with cash prizes—that she was not allowed to enter them. So she found other ways to make money with a gun. She became a market hunter, selling wild fowl, mostly pheasant and turkey, to shopkeepers in Greenville, Ohio.

From Katzenberger's General Store in Greenville, Annie's birds went to hotels in Cincinnati, eighty miles away. There they were

# TURKEY SHOOT

## A turkeyshoot does not involve real turkeys.

THE MAIN GOAL IS TO SHOOT ON OR CLOSE TO THE BULLSEYE ON A PAPER TARGET. EACH CONTESTANT SHOOTS FROM A DISTANCE OF 58 FEET IN A SERIES OF ROUNDS. THE TARGETS ARE THEN JUDGED AND THE WINNER IS DETERMINED BY WHO SHOOTS THE CLOSEST TO THE BULLSEYE.

served up in style in the hotel dining rooms.

In the early 1870s, most hunters used shot-guns, which fired pellets of buckshot. Birds killed this way were riddled with shot. Diners had to pick out the tiny pellets as they ate, the way they picked bones out of fish or seeds out of fruit. They were used to it, but it was annoying.

Parker Brothers
16·gauge Shotgun

100 Brass Shells

The only gun Annie had was a rifle, which fired one bullet at a time. Her aim was so good that she needed only one bullet to bring down a bird. That bullet could be removed easily before the game was cooked and served.

Annie's skill made everyone happy: the diners were happy because they could eat their pheasant without swallowing buckshot; the hotels, because serving such deluxe game attracted customers; the Katzenberger brothers, because they sold Annie's game at a good price; and Annie herself, because for the first time in her life she could actually save money.

The nickels and dimes she earned with her shooting added up. One day, they paid off the $200 mortgage on her family's new house.

"My heart leaped with joy," she wrote later, "as

I handed the money to Mother."

Annie was fifteen years old.

# Chapter 4
# Annie and Frank and Dear Old George

Jack Frost managed one of the Cincinnati hotels that served Annie's game. He was intrigued by the fact that this small, soft-spoken backwoods girl was a crack shot. He came up with the idea of putting her in a shooting match.

The cash prize of $100 (a huge sum in those days) was an irresistible challenge to Annie. It was certainly a far cry from the local turkey shoots she knew so well. What she didn't know was that she'd be competing against a professional sharpshooter.

Her opponent was a man in his twenties named Frank Butler. Frank traveled around the country giving shooting exhibitions in vaudeville houses— theaters that offered shooting acts, minstrel shows, and short plays as entertainment. He liked to challenge local champions to outdoor shooting matches, and boasted that he could beat almost anyone.

He wasn't expecting a fifteen-year-old girl.

"I nearly dropped dead when a little slim girl in short dresses stepped up to the mark with me," he said later.

As the crowd watched, he and Annie began shooting. Taking turns, they hit each of their flying targets perfectly. It looked as if the contest might be a tie. Then Frank missed his last shot of the match.

Now it was Annie's turn. "My knees were shaking," she wrote. But she aimed, fired, and hit. She had a perfect score of twenty-five out of twenty-five.

She won the match, and she also won Frank Butler's heart. As the two parted company, Frank gave Annie, her sister Lydia,

and her brother-in-law Joe free passes to his show.

There they watched Frank shoot an apple off the head of his poodle, George.

When George brought Annie a piece of the apple, she sent back a thank-you note. Frank and George responded by sending Annie a box of candy.

Less than a year later, Frank and Annie were married. George sat and watched, wagging his tail.

There are many colorful stories about Annie's first stage appearance. One says that when Frank's partner, John Graham, fell ill, Annie offered to take his place. Once onstage, she surprised Frank. He wasn't expecting her to shoot—he thought she would be too shy. But she insisted on taking every other shot, and never missed once. The audience loved it.

Another story says that when Annie stepped in for John Graham, she simply threw targets—glass balls and clay pigeons—for Frank to shoot. Frank missed so often—perhaps because he was facing Annie, not John—that a man in the audience shouted, "Let the girl shoot!"

So Annie picked up a gun, made the shots, and began her life in show business. Or so the story goes.

We do know that in 1883, Annie and Frank toured the Midwest with a sharpshooting act they called "Butler and Oakley." By day they did shooting exhibitions. By night they played in vaudeville theaters.

The former Phoebe Ann Moses (or Mozee, which she preferred) had taken a new name to go along with her new career. Now, as

The
AMAZING
GIUSEPPE
BROTHERS

Annie Oakley, she also began taking more of the spotlight.

She shot glass balls and clay pigeons. She shot standing up and sitting down and over her shoulder. And now it was Annie, not Frank, who aimed at "dear old George" and shot an apple "from between his soft ears."

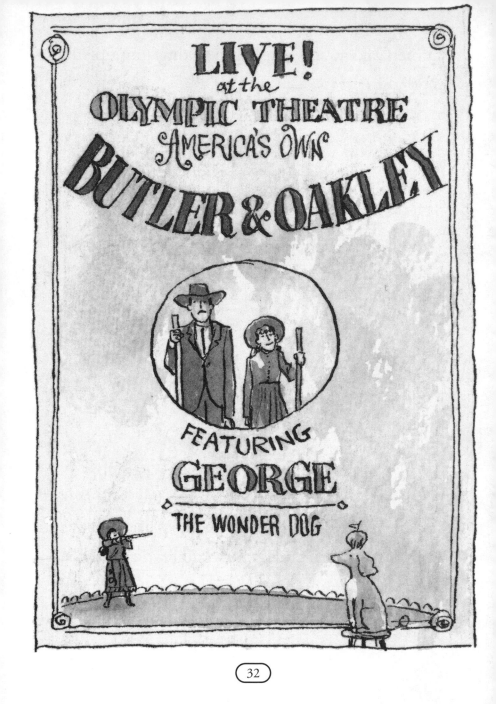

Frank Butler was quick to see that Annie was a far better shot than he was. He also saw that Annie had what it took to be a great performer. Her easy, high-spirited stage presence charmed audiences. But it was her dainty, ladylike appearance, combined with her dazzling shooting skill, that won the crowds over so completely. Spectators might stare in disbelief when the tiny, slim, dark-haired Annie skipped onstage. But by the time she made her final curtsy, they were always on their feet, cheering.

With a new marriage, a new name, and a new career, Annie's life was good. In 1884 it got even better: She and Frank joined the circus.

# Chapter 5
# Little Sure Shot

"A whole world of wonders! Greater than the greatest!" boasted an 1884 ad for the Sells Brothers Circus. Barnum and Bailey might have been bigger, but only the Sells Brothers had two hippos, a trained elk, a five-ton, three-horned rhinoceros,

Miss Maggie Claire, the Flying Woman, and an entire herd of zebras.

It also had the "champion rifle shots" Butler and Oakley. Annie and Frank quit the adults-only world of vaudeville. They wanted to be in the circus, which offered wholesome family entertainment. So they signed forty-week contracts and arranged to meet up with the Sells Brothers in April.

A few weeks before joining the circus, Annie and Frank had been appearing at a vaudeville theater in St. Paul, Minnesota. Annie's performance that night went as it usually did: She skipped onstage, shot corks out of bottles, snuffed candles by shooting out their flames, and shot off the burning end of a cigarette from Frank's mouth. The audience clapped and cheered and left the theater.

But one man was so impressed with Annie's shooting that he demanded to meet her right away. He was Sitting Bull, the great Sioux chief who was famous for defeating General George Armstrong Custer at Little Bighorn in 1876.

# Little Bighorn

CREE

BLACKFOOT

OJIBWA

CROW X

BATTLE OF
LITTLE BIGHORN

SANTEE

CHEYNNE

## DAKOTA (SIOUX) TERRITORY

OSAGE

KIOWA

COMANCHE

**S**ITTING BULL SAW A VISION OF A VICTORIOUS BATTLE AT LITTLE BIGHORN.

LT. COL. GEORGE A. CUSTER DEFIANTLY LED HIS UNIT OF 215 MEN TOWARD THE MIDDLE OF THE LARGEST INDIAN CAMP IN THE SIOUX NATION. CUSTER'S UNIT WAS OUTNUMBERED AND NO MATCH FOR THE INDIANS LED BY CHIEF CRAZY HORSE.

NO PRISONERS WERE TAKEN.

Now it was 1884, and the worst of the government's battles with the Indian tribes were over. Sitting Bull was technically a prisoner of war. He was also a famed leader and a powerful, striking figure. He had been invited to the theater that night by a city official. But it was not until Annie started shooting that Sitting Bull paid any attention to the show.

Annie agreed to meet Sitting Bull the next day. After exchanging photographs, the chief presented Annie with many gifts. He even gave her the moccasins he had worn when he fought Custer. He told Annie of the daughter he had lost after the Battle of Little Bighorn, and declared that Annie could replace her. If Annie came to his territory, he said, she would be welcomed as a princess.

Annie was surprised and flattered. "The old man was so pleased with me," she wrote, "he insisted upon adopting me, and I was then and there christened 'Watanya Cicilla,' or 'Little Sure Shot.'"

Annie liked her new name. It was in keeping with the way the public saw her, as a woman of the West— even though she had never been west of Kansas.

She already wore a Western-style hat with a silver star. Now her beautiful costumes began to take on a Western flavor also. She added fringe, embroidered flowers, and beadwork.

Like most Westerners, Annie knew how to ride, but now she taught herself how to shoot from horseback. Riding both sidesaddle and astride, she made shooting from a horse look as easy as the rest of her act. At her prompting, the Sells Brothers program referred to Butler and Oakley as "The Great Far West Rifle Shots."

Annie made her entrance on horseback, blowing kisses and smiling. Then she hit every target that Frank released—at a gallop. The crowds were dazzled. Everyone knew that cowboys and Indians out on the Western plains could shoot like that, but a woman?

Annie's showmanship was becoming as skillful as her shooting. In her private life, she was still a modest, soft-spoken Ohio native, the daughter of Quakers. Onstage she was a hard-riding, fast-shooting cowgirl in petticoats, and she was a big hit.

In 1885, she and Frank moved on from the Sells Brothers Circus. That spring they joined the grandest traveling spectacle of the century— Buffalo Bill's Wild West show.

# Chapter 6
# Welcome to the Wild West

William F. Cody, known as Buffalo Bill, was a tall, imposing man with shoulder-length hair. As a young man, he had been a Pony Express rider, an army scout, and a stagecoach driver. Then the Kansas Pacific Railroad hired him to supply buffalo meat to its track workers. He killed more than 4,000 buffalo in eight months, and from that time on he was called Buffalo Bill.

Luckily for the buffalo, Bill decided his good looks and outgoing personality belonged on the stage. He headed east, first to Chicago and then to New York, and appeared in many plays about the Western frontier. It was ten years before he found his true calling as a producer.

Bill saw that audiences all over America were curious about the Wild West, so he designed a show—part rodeo, part circus, part theater—that would give them a taste of it.

The show was advertised as "A Visit to the Wild West in Three Hours," and it kept its promise. With a huge cast of American cowboys; Mexican cowboys (called vaqueros); Indians; and hundreds of animals,

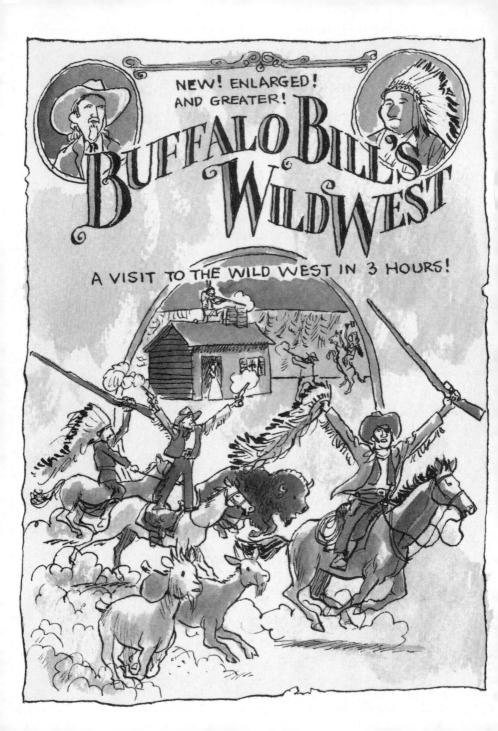

including horses, goats, and elk, it was a fast, noisy, thrilling mix of shooting, roping, lariat tricks, music, and showy horsemanship.

Most exciting of all were the reenactments of historic frontier events. Bill made sure they were authentic, down to the last detail. A maestro in buckskin, he directed the cast, designed the costumes, and staged the action for maximum effect.

Crowds could see real Pony Express riders changing horses in mid-gallop. They could see fierce outlaws ambushing the famous Deadwood coach. They could see Pawnee and Sioux Indians attacking and burning settlers' cabins—and then shout with relief when Buffalo Bill and his fearless posse came to the rescue with guns blazing.

Everyone who saw it agreed that the Wild West show was an unforgettable experience—well worth the ticket price of fifty cents.

Annie and Frank knew that the Wild West

show was the perfect place for Annie's talent to shine. But when she and Frank approached Bill, he turned them down. He already had plenty of sharpshooters, he said. Besides, Annie was asking for a lot of money—five times as much as his cowboys got.

Annie was crushed. But she was also determined. So she sent him a proposal. "We would join them, give three exhibitions, and if, after the

third one, they did not think me worth the price, the three days would be free, and I would join another company," she wrote.

It was a good offer, and Bill took her up on it. Could she and Frank join the show in Louisville, Kentucky, for a few days? Indeed they could. But when Annie and Frank showed up at the Louisville Baseball Park, the field was deserted. Bill, perhaps forgetting his appointment, was leading the show on a parade through the city.

Annie decided to practice her act on the base-ball field. When she finished, a man in a suit and a derby hat ran across the baseball diamond to her.

"Fine! Wonderful!" he cried enthusiastically. "Have you got some photographs with your gun?"

The man was Bill's partner, Nate Salsbury. He hired Annie on the spot.

# Chapter 7
# An Uncommon Life

It is safe to say that no other woman of her time had a daily routine like Annie's. On a typical day with the Wild West show, she woke at five A.M. in a tent. Then she "took a morning dip like a wild bird" in a collapsible bathtub. After putting on her traveling clothes—a gown with matching cape and gloves—she boarded the special show train with Frank and the other performers.

When the group reached their next stop, Annie's tent was waiting for her. It was furnished with folding chairs, a table, chintz curtains, two cots, many satin pillows, and a carpet strewn with cougar skins. It was not feminine in the conventional sense—a large gun rack stood in the corner—but it was cozy and comfortable. Annie and Frank always preferred it to a hotel.

After a hearty lunch, Annie spent the afternoon rehearsing. Then she had a witch-hazel rubdown and a nap. "Rolled in a soft blanket, I lay me down in a hammock to sleep," she wrote, "lulled by the wind."

Then came dinner, an hour of writing, some lariat practice, and the evening's performance.

Annie appeared early in the show. Bill believed that her act, which was exciting but in no way frightening, would prepare the audience for the hair-raising commotion—smoke, noise, and Indian war whoops—that came later. As *The New York Times* said, "Women and children see a harmless woman there, and they do not get worried."

Far from being worried, people were awestruck. Annie's act was only ten minutes long, but it was unforgettable.

She skipped into the arena gaily, blowing kisses to the audience. She wore her Western-style hat pinned with the silver star. Her Western styled dresses, usually blue or brown cotton, had white starched collars and the skirts were embroidered by Annie herself. She also made her own pearl-buttoned leggings—they had to fit perfectly.

Her girlish costume and her lighthearted entrance were meant to be misleading. Annie looked like a schoolgirl, but the moment she picked up her gun, she was all business.

After choosing one of the many rifles and shotguns from a table in the arena, she gave the signal and Frank started releasing targets. Clay birds flew into the air, first singly, then in pairs, then in threes and fours. As fast as they came, Annie hit them all.

Then she shot glass balls, sometimes fifty or sixty in a row. If she missed, she scowled and stamped her foot. Then she would quickly do a much harder stunt—perhaps lying on her back across a chair and shooting a target upside down—just to show the audience that she had missed on purpose.

She could toss two balls into the air at the same time, twirl around, and hit them both. She could hit a target behind her by looking in a mirror or even a knife blade. She could shoot right- and left-handed at the same time—she did this with pistols. And she could break eleven glass balls, using five different guns, in ten seconds. It was no wonder that newspapers called her everything from "most marvelous" to "astonishing."

The public had never seen anything like her.

# Chapter 8
# The Island and the Garden

By the end of the 1885 season, Bill and his partner, Nate, believed Annie was bringing them luck. The Wild West show was finally making a profit, in part because Annie's popularity was growing. She wasn't yet a star, but she was fast becoming a main attraction.

She even drew Sitting Bull to the show. At first the chief had refused to sign on, but when he learned that Annie was working for Buffalo Bill, he changed his mind.

If he could see Machin Chilla Watanya Cicilla ("my daughter, Little Sure Shot") every day, he would join the company. "Then he picked his braves and the contract was signed," wrote Annie. The chief had become "a dear, faithful old friend" to her.

One person who was most surely not Annie's friend was a fifteen-year-old sharpshooter from California called Lillian Smith. Bill liked the idea of two lady shooters, and he hired Lillian without telling Annie. Worse, when Lillian arrived, she told anybody who would listen that "Annie Oakley is done for."

Annie was a very competitive person. She didn't blame Lillian for wanting to win. But Lillian's rudeness offended her. It forced her into an unfriendly rivalry, and into the only lie she ever told about herself. From 1885 on, both Annie and Frank claimed that Annie was six years younger than she was. As far as the world knew, she was twenty, not twenty-six—nearly as young as Lillian.

And a better shot, of course.

In the summer of 1886, Bill booked the show into a huge arena on Staten Island, New York. On the day of their arrival, the entire company was going to ride down Manhattan, from Forty-second Street to the Battery. Annie was seriously ill with blood poisoning, but she insisted on riding in the parade, despite Frank's objections.

"I had so
carefully planned
and fitted a pretty habit
with everything to match," she

wrote. "That parade in New York meant everything to me."

And as she well knew, her rival, Lillian Smith, would be riding in it. Ill or not, Annie was going to appear. She managed to get through the long ride, and then collapsed for four days. It was the only time she ever missed a show. Nevertheless, she was soon back in the spotlight more than ever. New Yorkers swarmed to Staten Island on ferries from morning till night. Annie and the rest of the troupe performed before 15,000 to 20,000 people every day that summer. The Wild West Show became the most popular entertainment in New York history.

With success like that, Bill reasoned, there was no reason to leave New York. When winter came,

the show could simply play indoors. There was a large, imposing brick-and-marble building on lower Fifth Avenue that had hosted concerts, boxing matches, and the Barnum and Bailey Circus. It was called Madison Square Garden, and it would be perfect.

Like Annie, Bill was always striving to top himself. So he hired a writer called Steele MacKaye to turn the Wild West show into a play. The result was a four-act extravaganza called "Drama of Civilization." It was performed against colorful painted sets, under a roof that had been raised

twenty-five feet, to guard against stray bullets. It even had a giant blower that whipped up prairie "cyclones."

Annie's new act was one of the highlights of the show. In addition to shooting from the ground, she also did some spectacular stunts on horseback.

Riding at a gallop, she slid down to untie a handkerchief from her horse's rear leg. Then she picked up a handkerchief, her whip, and her hat from the ground the same way. These stunts won her a gold medal from the Ladies Riding Club of New York.

One stunt of Annie's never made the newspapers. It was a ride she took one snowy afternoon between performances. She slipped out of the

Garden, hitched a large moose to a sled, and drove him around the block. The moose, called Jerry, turned out to be hungry. "All went swimmingly until . . . Jerry's beadlike eyes espied a pushcart laden with nice, juicy, red apples," wrote Annie. "Three of his long strides and he was at the cart, and apples flew in all directions. The vendor's hair stood straight on end. My moose ate the apples and my $5 paid the bill."

Once forced to watch every penny, Annie could now spend money freely, even on a hungry moose. She had come a long way.

# Chapter 9
# England

In the spring of 1887, Annie sailed to England for Queen Victoria's Golden Jubilee. Victoria had been queen for fifty years, and the jubilee was a national celebration. There were fairs, parades, and public entertainments of all kinds.

Bill managed to book the Wild West show in London for the entire summer. It was one of the smartest things he ever did.

In true Wild West style, even the troupe's

Then the show's Sioux and Pawnee Indians boarded. They were not happy—they believed that an ocean crossing spelled almost certain doom. To everyone's surprise, their fears came true. A few days out at sea, a ferocious storm hit the ship.

As the Indians huddled together singing their death chants, Annie rode out the storm wrapped in an oilskin and strapped to a chair.

"Not a passenger except my husband and myself knew that we had been in danger of losing our lives," she wrote. The storm was so fierce that the ship lost a propeller and drifted 250 miles off course.

departure was a spectacle. As a crowd watched from the docks, the entire Deadwood stagecoach was boxed and loaded into the hold of a steamship.

Then came buffalo, deer, bears, elks, donkeys, mules, 180 horses, and five Texas steer. Buffalo Bill strode up and down the deck shouting orders, and the Western and Mexican cowboys came aboard next. They were in high spirits.

When the steamship finally docked in London, it got a warm welcome. Frank had become an expert at getting publicity for Annie. He made sure that Wild West posters were plastered all over the city. When the show opened on May 9, more than 10,000 people were packed into the grandstands. All of London wanted to see "the Yankeeries," as the Americans were called.

And they liked what they saw. From its very first day, the show was a great success. It went on to attract more than half a million people that month alone. Among them was Prince Edward, the future king of England.

At the special show for Edward (called a command performance), "we all worked like little hound pups at a rabbit hole," wrote Annie. The prince found the show so exciting that he stood for most of it. He was especially impressed with Annie, and had her called to the royal box. Wanting to congratulate her, the prince held out his hand. In a surprising gesture, Annie shook the hand of Edward's wife, Princess Alexandra, instead.

"You'll have to excuse me, please," she said sweetly to the prince. "I'm an American, and in America, ladies come first."

Much was made of Annie's "mistake" in the newspapers the next day. But she knew exactly what she was doing. The prince liked to flirt, and Annie knew that it pained Alexandra. Her sympathies were with the princess, and this was her way of showing it.

Edward took no offense. "What a pity there are not more women in the world like that little one," he remarked. Soon after he wrote to Bill. Would "Annie Oakley, the little girl who shoots so cleverly in your show," agree to a shooting match against Grand Duke Michael of Russia?

Annie must have been pleased that Edward had singled her out rather than Lillian Smith. She accepted and beat the duke.

Her next royal encounter pleased Annie even more. Queen Victoria had been in mourning since the death of her beloved husband, Albert, in 1861. She appeared in public to unveil memorials to him; otherwise, her people almost never saw her. So it astonished London when the queen, like every other man, woman, and child in the city, decided that she had to see the Wild West show.

On the day of the command performance, Victoria arrived promptly at five. She took her seat in a box filled with flowers and draped with crimson velvet. Bill opened the show by saluting her from his prancing white mustang. Then Indians in full battle dress and lariat-twirling cowboys rode past, whooping their greetings. The woman who had been wearing black for seventeen years began to have a good time.

She especially enjoyed Annie's performance, and called for her "with a little nod and a wave of her hand." She asked Annie many questions about her life and career, and told her she was "a very, very clever little girl."

"To be called 'clever' by Queen Victoria meant the highest compliment," Annie wrote proudly. It was the high point of her visit.

Annie became a star during her six-month stay in London. People greeted her by name when she took her morning ride in Hyde Park. London society invited her to lunches, teas, and dinners. Bootblacks and newsboys called her the "boss shooter." Though she made no secret of the fact that she was happily married, more than one count proposed marriage. She even inspired a

novel called *Rifle Queen, Annie Oakley*. It was sixty-four pages of whopping lies and wild stories, and the public loved it.

Annie also established herself as a world-class markswoman in London. The Notting Hill Gun Club, a group of the best shots in England, presented her with a large gold medal—the only one it ever awarded. The London gunmaker Charles Lancaster admired Annie's shooting so much that he designed and made a group of lightweight guns just for her.

By now, Annie far outshone Lillian Smith, though Lillian insisted on equal billing with Annie, and got it. However, a newspaper story reported that Lillian was cheating in her act. It said that she was lying about both the speed and the accuracy of her shooting. Annie kept silent. She may have suspected all along that Lillian was dishonest, but she was above saying so.

At the same time, Annie's relationship with Bill grew tense. Perhaps he resented her popularity, which now was greater than his. He certainly ignored the stories about Lillian Smith, and treated her as Annie's equal. To Annie, this must have seemed very unfair.

As ladylike as ever, Annie said nothing about her differences with Bill. But at the end of the London season, she and Frank left the show.

# Chapter 10
# Europe

Annie and Frank worried over their decision, but it proved to be a good one. The public wanted to see Annie Oakley, whether she was with Buffalo Bill's show or not. She returned to America a star.

For the next year and a half, she entered dozens of shooting matches. She won most of them, and a great deal of prize money, too. Then she took the lead in a play called "Deadwood Dick: or The Sunbeam of the Sierras." As Sunbeam, she played a pioneer girl captured and raised by Indians. She ended the show by shooting a dozen glass balls before running offstage in a cloud of smoke.

"I never understood why the press abstained from vegetable throwing," she wrote, "but they threw not one carrot." As usual, Annie was being modest. Reporters wouldn't dream of throwing anything at Annie. They loved her.

Annie never spoke about her difficulties with Buffalo Bill. She kept silent when they were smoothed over, in 1889. It was probably no coincidence that she agreed to come back to his show the year Lillian Smith left.

Bill was taking everyone to Paris, and he wanted Annie to come along. He expected a successful run there, as good as the one in London. It was an appealing prospect for everybody, including Annie and Frank.

But on opening night, 20,000 Parisians watched the ambush of the Deadwood stage and the burning of settlers' cabins in chilly silence. These scenes, so popular in America and England, left them cold. Bill realized that the French knew very little about American history (or the English language) and might not understand—or enjoy— a great deal of the show. He was faced with the awful possibility that Paris would be a flop.

Then Annie appeared in the arena. Her brilliant shooting needed no translation; it spoke for itself. And it dazzled the French, who soon were cheering wildly. By the next day, Annie was the talk of Paris. Thanks to her, the six-month French run was a success, and she herself was adored.

When Bill decided to take the show on a three-year tour of Europe, Annie and Frank decided to go, too.

Annie was not a typical American tourist. In Munich, she saved a Bavarian prince's life by hauling him out of the path of a runaway horse. In Venice, she rode in a gondola full of American Indians. In Vienna, she met Franz Joseph I, the emperor of Austria and Hungary. Seeing his lined, worried face, she wrote, "I decided that being plain little Annie Oakley with 10 minutes' work

twice a day was good enough for me, for at least I had my freedom."

Of course, she wasn't "plain little Annie Oakley" anymore. Annie was now a celebrity. News of her traveled fast and far, and when a French newspaper mistakenly reported that she was dead, the story spread quickly. Within days, it appeared in papers all over Europe and America. "Poor Anne Oakley Dies in a Foreign Land—the Greatest of Female Shots," read the headline in one Ohio newspaper.

The News
JANUARY 2, 1891
ANNIE OAKLEY
DEAD!
FOUND DEAD
IN A FORIEGN
LAND
STAR OF BUFFALO BILL'S
WILD WEST SHOW

When Susan Moses heard the news, she collapsed with grief. Bill Cody, in America for the winter, was shocked and puzzled. He quickly cabled Frank in England. Frank sent a reassuring reply, and Bill responded, "I am so glad our Annie ain't dead, ain't you?"

WESTERN UNION
TELEGRAM

BILL CODY
UNITED STATES
(AMERICA)

I AM SO GLAD OUR ANNIE
AIN'T DEAD AIN'T YOU

BILL

# Chapter 11
# America

Bill's show took up fourteen acres at Chicago's Columbian Exposition of 1893. With the exception of a belly dancer called "Little Egypt, Darling of the Nile," it was definitely the fair's most popular attraction, drawing up to 22,000 people at a time.

It now featured military riders from many countries— Russian Cossacks, American cavalrymen, English lancers, and French dragoons—along with the original cowboys and Indians.

There were more than 100 American Indians. There were Argentine *gauchos* and Mexican *vaqueros*. There were Arab riders in flowing robes.

But Annie got top billing. As the star attraction, she appeared first on the program, wearing one of her thirty-five hand-sewn and embroidered costumes. With her long curls and her trademark Western hat, she still looked girlish, though now she was thirty-three years old.

Her performance was as thrilling as ever. It featured many familiar stunts—shooting the end off a lit cigarette, "scrambling" eggs by shooting a bunch of them as they flew through the air—and a few new ones. One of these, slicing a playing card in half lengthwise with a pistol shot, was so difficult that few attempted it. Annie made it a regular feature of her act.

The Wild West show was seen by an estimated six million people that summer, and cleared a million dollars, breaking records for both attendance and profit. As for Annie, she was now one of the best-known women in America.

By Christmas 1893, Annie and Frank had moved into a roomy new house in Nutley, New Jersey. For the first time in her life, Annie had a housekeeper. She decided she wanted guests, too, so she sent a letter of invitation to *Forest & Stream* magazine.

"I beg of all friends and sportsmen not to pass by without stopping," she wrote. "No matter if they shoot a $30 or a $300 gun, their welcome will be just the same."

Her offer delighted the magazine's readers. But if any of them stopped by in March 1894, they wouldn't find Annie at home. She was back in a tent again—this time a circus tent.

The Nutley Amateur Circus was a charity event, put on to benefit the Red Cross. Frank, who helped organize the circus, had no trouble persuading Annie to appear. Both she and Frank had happy memories of their days with the Sells Brothers. And the Red Cross was one of their favorite charities.

As always, Annie pushed herself to improve her act. She already could shoot from horseback. Why not shoot standing, riding bareback? In Nutley, she did just that. As the horse cantered around the ring, Annie kept her balance perfectly, and hit every target Frank released into the air. She never had done the stunt in public before. It alone, said one newspaper, was worth the trip to New Jersey.

Meanwhile, Nate Salsbury and Bill were in Brooklyn, getting ready for another Wild West season. It was a huge job. The show had grown so big that a special arena had to be built for it.

As construction began, the twenty-four-acre show lot became a tent city, filled with cowboys, Indians, stagehands, animal handlers, musicians, blacksmiths, porters, cooks, and a small army of roughriders from all over the world.

By May, the arena was complete. It measured 450 feet by 312 feet, and was decorated with a giant panorama of the Western mountains. Thomas Edison's company installed the lighting system. It was expensive—$30,000— but Bill was sure it was

worth the money. For the first time, the show could play outdoors at night. With extra evening shows, profits could be greater than ever before.

The show was splendid, and Annie's performances were wonderful. But Bill's hopes were dashed. The country was suffering a depression, and many people couldn't afford show tickets. Attendance was so poor that the show was in debt by the end of the season.

The only solution, announced Bill, was to go on the road again.

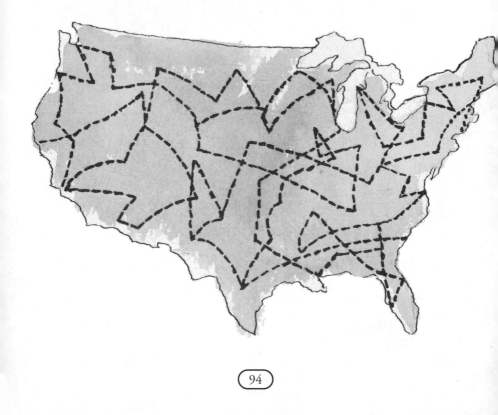

For the next five years, Annie and Frank saw little of their dream house in New Jersey. They spent most of their time traveling with the show, which now was managed by James Bailey of circus fame.

Bailey made changes. He added circus acts. He changed the show's schedule so that it traveled from town to town in a series of one-night stands. Like Ringling Brothers and Barnum and Bailey, which Bailey also managed, the Wild West show now played between 100 and 130 American cities a season. With constant travel, there was almost no time to rest.

Once again, Annie and Frank made their home in the big canvas tent, with its collapsible bathtub and gun racks. If Annie was less than happy with life on the road, she never complained. She was used to hard work; she had been working hard since childhood. And she never had expected her life to be glamorous.

Bill grumbled to reporters and threatened to retire. Annie, always a lady, said everything was fine. If she had to get rain-soaked every now and then, or shoot in ankle-deep mud, so what? Things could have been a lot worse.

# Chapter 12
# Her Own Woman

In the early morning of October 28, 1901, the Wild West show was traveling by train from North Carolina to Virginia. There it would play its final date of the season. The troupe was weary. Everybody was ready to say their good-byes and take a long break for the winter.

Frank and Annie were fast asleep in their stateroom. Suddenly they were wakened by the screech of brakes. Then, before they could even speak, they were thrown from their beds. It was pitch black. There were cries, shouts, and then the terrible sound of animals screaming. The show train had crashed. A freight train had hit it head-on.

Dozens of performers were injured in the wreck, which killed 110 horses and destroyed five show cars.

Frank was not hurt, but Annie suffered serious injuries to her hands and back. She spent months in a New Jersey hospital, recovering, and thinking about her future.

After seventeen years with the Wild West show, longer than any other performer, Annie realized that she wanted to do other things with her life. She and Frank agreed that it was time to leave the show.

When she was well again, Annie took the lead in a play called "The Western Girl." She played Nancy, the virtuous daughter of a bandit. Like the earlier "Deadwood Dick," "The Western Girl" was written for Annie, which meant that she did more shooting than acting. Whiskey bottles,

lanterns, glass balls, and villains all felt the sting of her bullets.

Her reviews were good, but this was nothing new: Annie's reviews were always good. Though she was modest about praise from reporters, she was pleased that they treated her well. She had even come to expect it.

Then a news story calling her a drug user was published in 1903. "Annie Oakley Begs Court For Mercy: Famous Woman Crack Shot . . . Steals to Secure Cocaine," read one headline. "Annie Oakley in Prison, Famous

Rifle Shot of Buffalo Bill's Show a Cocaine Victim," read another.

Annie was horrified. She wrote to the newspapers immediately. She was not in prison. The drug addict who had used her name falsely was exposed. It was time to set the record straight. To their credit, many newspapers quickly apologized in print.

But Annie was not satisfied. She had been careful to protect her good name all her life. She dressed properly. She did not drink, smoke, or curse. She might be a performer, but she was a respectable woman just the same. Apologies were not enough. Her wholesome image had been damaged.

Annie went on to sue dozens of newspapers for writing lies about her. She appeared in court twenty-five times to testify about her life and character. She always had charmed audiences; now she charmed juries also.

One after another, the courts concluded that Annie Oakley the sharpshooter was also a fine woman whose reputation had been hurt. They felt she should win her case—not for money or publicity, as one lawyer hinted, but to clear her name. Every jury decided in her favor.

Annie continued her battle with the press until the last suit was settled in 1910. Then she turned to a different cause. It was one that always had been dear to her heart. She would teach women how to shoot.

Annie had long believed that women should be able to handle guns "as naturally as they handle babies." She had learned to do both; why couldn't

others? She invited women to her shooting exhibitions, promising them a warm welcome. She wrote a series of how-to articles for the *New York Journal*. She told women that shooting was "one of the best kinds of tonics for the nerves and for the mind." Most important, it was an excellent way for them to protect themselves and their homes.

In Annie's time, this message was unusual. If there was a gun in the house, the man shot it. Men were the ones who hunted and who used guns for protection. Women relied on their men to protect them. But why? asked Annie. She believed women should rely on themselves.

Annie was at a resort hotel in North Carolina when she overheard a guest say, "My, how I wish I was a man so I could shoot."

She introduced herself and offered to give the woman a lesson. It must have been a good one. When it ended, Annie's new pupil had scored a bull's-eye.

From then on, Annie spent several hours a day teaching women at the resort's rifle ranges. She and Frank stayed in North Carolina for seven years. In that time, Annie taught 15,000 women how to shoot. And she did it for free.

Annie had grown up poor. So had Frank. After working hard and saving for most of their lives, they now found themselves wealthy. In retirement, they could do what they liked with their time and money. They chose to be generous.

Annie continued to give free shooting lessons to women. She appeared at many charity shows—for everything from the Red Cross to an agricultural school. She gave thousands of dollars to veterans' hospitals. She had her gold medals melted down and donated the money to the treatment of tuberculosis, a disease that had killed two of her sisters. And she very quietly paid for the educations of nineteen young women, all orphans.

When America entered World War I, Annie and Frank visited many army camps, giving

shooting exhibitions and talks. When the war ended, she peformed at a charity circus on Long Island to raise money for soldiers who had been wounded.

Annie was now sixty-two years old. Frank threw plates, glass balls, and other targets for his "crackshot Quaker wife." She hit every one.

That same year, Annie was hurt badly in a car accident in Florida. She never entirely recovered. In 1926, she died. Frank, her beloved husband and lifelong companion, died eighteen days later.

*They are buried side by side in a peaceful Ohio cemetery, a few miles from the place where Annie was born.*

# TIMELINE OF ANNIE OAKLEY'S LIFE

**1860** —— Annie (Phoebe Ann Moses) is born, August 13, in Ohio

**1866** —— Annie's father, Jacob Moses, dies

**1870** —— Annie is sent to work at the Darke County Infirmary

**1875** —— Annie returns home for her sister Lydia's wedding; she pays off the mortgage on the house with her shooting

**1875** —— Annie meets Frank Butler

**1876** —— Annie and Frank are married

**1883** —— Annie and Frank tour the Midwest as "Butler and Oakley"

**1884** —— Annie and Frank join the circus

**1885** —— Annie and Frank join Buffalo Bill's Wild West show

**1886** —— The Wild West show performs in New York

**1887** —— Annie sails to England for Queen Victoria's Golden Jubilee

**1889** —— Annie rejoins the Wild West show and travels to Paris

**1901** —— Wild West show train crash

**1903** —— Newspaper stories accuse Annie of drug use

**1917** —— Annie and Frank raise money for soldiers and perform for troops

**1926** —— Annie dies November 3, 18 days before Frank